NOTE TO PARENTS

My Book of Prayers is a selection of prayers chosen especially for children, based around different times, occasions and themes. Why not select a different prayer each day and choose a quiet time when you can pray with your child. Sharing this experience will help your child to understand that God does listen when we speak to him and that we can talk to God whoever we are and wherever we may be.

Every effort has been made to trace the author and owner of the copyright of these prayers. We offer our sincere apologies if we have used copyright material without due acknowledgement.

The *Gloria in Excelsis* (Glory to God in the Highest) is copyright © 1970, 1971, 1975, International Consultation on English Text (ICET) and is reproduced with permission.

My Book of Prayers

selected by Marjorie Newman
illustrated by Dianne Stuchbury

Copyright © 1990 World International Publishing Limited.
All rights reserved.
Published in Great Britain by World International Publishing Limited,
An Egmont Company, Egmont House,
P.O. Box 111, Great Ducie Street,
Manchester M60 3BL.
Printed in DDR.
ISBN 0 7235 4468 9

A CIP catalogue record for this book is available from the British Library

God's Love and Care

I thank You, Father, that You
listen to me.
I know You always listen to me.

John II: verses 41, 42

Make us brave to conquer fear,
Make us happy, full of cheer,
Sure that You are always near.
Hear us, Holy Father.

Thomas Benson Pollock, 1836–96
(slightly adapted)

Alone with none but You, my God,
I journey on my way.
What need I fear when Thou art near,
O King of night and day?
More safe am I within Thy hand
Than if a host did round me stand.

Saint Columba, 521–597

Into Your loving care,
Into Your keeping,
God who is everywhere,
Take us, we pray.

Anon

God bless all those that I love.
God bless all those that love me.
God bless all those that love
those that I love,
And all those that love those who love me.

New England Sampler

God bless us, everyone!

"Christmas Carol", Charles Dickens, 1812–70

For friends and grass and trees
We thank You, Lord above.
For smiling flowers and earth,
And sunny skies above.

We know Your tender love.
We thank You for Your care,
For light, and fields, and flowers,
And all things everywhere.

Anon

God is in Heaven.
Does He care,
Or is He good to me?
Yes, all I have, and all I love,
It's God that gives it me.

Thank You, God!

Anne Gilbert, 1782–1866
(adapted)

Thanks for Nature

For air and sunshine pure and sweet
We thank our Heavenly Father.

For grass that grows beneath our feet
We thank our Heavenly Father.

For leafy trees with fruit and shade
We thank our Heavenly Father.

For things of beauty He has made
We thank our Heavenly Father.

Anon

We thank Thee, Lord, for this fair earth,
The glittering sky, the silver sea.
For all their beauty, all their worth,
Their light and glory, come from Thee.

George Edward Lynch Cotton, 1813–66

Now thank we all our God,
With hearts and hands and voices,
Who wondrous things hath done,
In whom His world rejoices.

Martin Rinkart, 1586–1649
(translated by Catherine Winkworth, 1829-78)

For all things fair we hear or see,
Father in Heaven, we thank Thee.

Ralph Waldo Emerson, 1803–82

HARVEST

All good gifts around us
Are sent from Heaven above.
Then thank the Lord, O thank the Lord,
For all His love.

Matthias Claudius, 1740–1815
(translated by Jane Montgomery Campbell, 1817–78)

Come, ye thankful people, come,
Raise the song of harvest home:
All is safely gathered in,
Ere the winter storms begin.

Henry Alford, 1810–71

ANIMALS

Hey all you children,
Bless you the Lord!
All fathers and mothers,
Sisters and brothers,
Praise Him and magnify Him for ever!

All you deeps of the ocean,
Praise you the Lord!
All whales and porpoises,
Turtles and tortoises,
Praise Him and magnify Him for ever!

All field mice and larder mice,
Praise you the Lord!
All hedgehogs and voles,
Rabbits and moles,
Praise Him and magnify Him for ever!

Let everything that hath life
Praise the Lord!

Anon

He prayeth well who loveth well
Both man, and bird, and beast.
He prayeth best who loveth best
All things both great and small;
For the dear God who loveth us,
He made and loveth all.

Samuel Taylor Coleridge, 1772–1834

Dear Father hear and bless
Thy beasts and singing birds,
And guard with tenderness
Small things that have no words.

Anon

GRACE

Thank You for the world so sweet,
Thank You for the food we eat,
Thank You for the birds that sing,
Thank You, God, for everything.

E Rutter Leatham, 1870–1933

Father we thank Thee for the night,
And for the pleasant morning light.
For rest and food, and loving care
And all that makes the day so fair.

Rebecca J Weston
(circa 1890)

Thanks and Praise

It is a good thing to give thanks
unto the Lord, and to sing praises
to Your name, O Most High.

Psalm 92: verse 1

Let us with a gladsome mind
Praise the Lord, for He is kind.
For His mercies aye endure,
Ever faithful ever sure.

John Milton, 1608–74

We praise You, God, for things we see,
The growing flowers, the waving tree,
Our mother's face, the bright blue sky,
Where birds and clouds go floating by.
We praise You, God, for seeing.

Maria Matilda Penstone, 1859–1910
(slightly adapted)

All things praise Thee, Lord most high!
Heaven and earth and sea and sky!

Time and space are praising Thee!
All things praise Thee; Lord, may we!

George William Conder, 1821–74
(adapted)

Praise God from whom all blessings flow,
Praise Him all creatures here below,

Thomas Ken, 1637–1711

Praise Him, praise Him, all ye little children,
He is love, He is love!
Thank Him, thank Him, all ye little children,
He is love, He is love!

Anon
(circa 1890)

Father we thank Thee for the night,
And for the pleasant morning light,
For rest and food and loving care,
And all that makes the day so fair.

Help us to do the things we should,
To be to others kind and good.
In all we do in work or play,
To grow more loving every day.

Rebecca J Weston
(circa 1890)

Glory to God in the highest,
and peace to his people on earth.

Lord God, heavenly King,
almighty God and Father,
we worship You, we give You thanks,
we praise You for Your glory.

Holy Communion A

The Lord's Prayer

Our Father, who art in Heaven,
Hallowed be Thy name.
Thy Kingdom come, Thy will be done
On earth, as it is in Heaven.
Give us this day our daily bread.
And forgive us our trespasses
As we forgive those who trespass against us.
And lead us not into temptation,
But deliver us from evil.
For Thine is the Kingdom, the power and
   the glory,
For ever and ever,
Amen.

Matthew 6:9-13

ME

Holy God who madest me
And all things else to worship Thee,
Keep me fit in mind and heart,
Body and soul, to do my part.
Fit to stand, fit to run,
Fit for sorrow, fit for fun,
Fit to work, fit to play,
Fit to face life day by day.
Holy God who madest me,
Make me fit to worship Thee.

Anon

Jesus, friend of little children
Be a friend to me.
Take my hand and ever keep me
Close to Thee.

Teach me how to grow in goodness
Daily as I grow.
You have been a child, and surely,
You must know.

Walter John Mathams, 1853–1931
(slightly adapted)

Lord, teach me what I need,
And teach me how to pray,
And do not let me talk to You
Not meaning what I say.

John Burton 1803–77
(slightly adapted)

Night Time

Day is done,
Gone the sun
From the lake,
From the hills,
From the sky.
Safely rest.
All is well.
God is nigh.

Anon

Glory to Thee my God this night
For all the blessings of the light.
Keep me, O keep me, King of Kings,
Beneath Thine own almighty wings.

Thomas Ken, 1637–1711

Lord, keep us safe this night,
Secure from all our fears.
May angels guard us while we sleep
Till morning light appears.

John Leland, 1754–1841

Now the day is over,
Night is drawing nigh,
Shadows of the evening
Steal across the sky.

Now the darkness gathers,
Stars their watches keep.
Birds and beasts and flowers
Soon will be asleep.

Through the long night-watches
May Thine angels spread
Their white wings above me,
Watching round my bed.

When the morning wakens,
Then may I arise,
Pure and fresh and sinless
In Your Holy eyes.

Sabine Baring-Gould, 1834–1924

Loving Shepherd of Thy sheep,
Keep Thy lamb in safety keep.
Nothing can Thy power withstand,
None can pluck me from Thy hand.

Loving Shepherd, ever near,
Teach Thy lamb Thy voice to hear.
Suffer not my steps to stray
From the straight and narrow way.

Jane E Leeson, 1807–82

Jesus, tender Shepherd, hear me,
Bless Thy little lamb tonight.
Through the darkness be Thou near me,
Keep me safe till morning light.

Mary Duncan, 1814–40

Goodnight! Goodnight!
Far flies the light,
But still God's love
Shall shine above,
Making all bright.
Goodnight! Goodnight!

Victor Hugo (translation), 1802–85

I am going to sleep.
I shut both my eyes.
God this night
Keep faithful watch over me.

Early Dutch settlers